LEARNING TO SUCCEED AND SUCCEEDING TO LEARN

The <u>Smart</u> Way to Earn Better
Grades in School

Christopher K. James

LEARNING TO SUCCEED
AND
SUCCEEDING TO LEARN

The <u>Smart</u> Way to Earn Better Grades in School

Christopher K. James

Learning to Succeed and Succeeding to Learn:
The Smart Way to Earn Better Grades in School

Library of Congress Control Number: 2008901491

ISBN: 978-0-6151-9241-3

Table of Contents

INTRODUCTION

If you're like me, you hate school. Period. There is nothing worse than the sinking feeling in your gut when summer is coming to a close and school is ready to start. It's torture. At that time of year, I usually begin to have terrible dreams every night of going to school on the first day, only to discover that I don't know where my classes are or that I forgot my schedule and I'm going to fail. On the other hand, there's no better feeling than starting summer vacation knowing that you don't have to worry one bit about school for over three months (unless, of course, summer school is involved, but that makes me shudder even more). Usually I store my backpack away without even taking the time to empty it, because, after all, it's summer and I can stop thinking about school.

If you're not like me, and I won't hold it against you if you're not, you like school. Maybe you love school. You like to see all of your classmates again. You're sick of all the boredom you had during the summer and are ready to get back into things. You love to learn and you feel that schoolwork is the best way to absorb everything you can.

Either way, you are reading this book for a reason. And that, I presume, is because you are not satisfied with the grades you're receiving. Maybe you've never really tried to do well in school and you've decided now's the time to start. Or, maybe you're trying very hard but nothing is coming of it. It may seem that others can get good grades no matter what, and you want to know how to become one of those people. No matter what your motivation is, you have come to the right source.

In today's competitive world, grades are becoming more and more important to weed out the successful from the unsuccessful. If you're in high school, your GPA can determine what scholarships you receive for college, or even whether you're accepted into your school of choice at all. If you're in college, employers are referring more and more to GPAs to choose applicants for entry-level positions. I'm sure you're in agreement that how well you do in school can pave the way for your future. This is exactly why you need to be in control of your education.

Even though I have always disliked school, I have somehow managed to succeed in ways that I never would have thought possible. I have gained several strategies that have greatly assisted me along the way and launched me toward success in my career. In order for you, too, to learn how to conquer your education, I would like to submit to you what I deem to be the smart way to earn better grades in school.

MOTIVATION

It is very important that you ask yourself the following questions: Do *I* really want to do better in school? Do *I* have the desire to try my best? If not, or if someone else is forcing you to read this book, then please do not continue. You will be wasting both your own time and mine. If you really want to do better in school, then it has to be your own decision. No one else can do it for you.

Now that I have warned you and you are ready to continue, I assume that you are sufficiently prepared to learn and apply the principles required to succeed in school. When you are self-motivated, little things make all the difference. For example, when *you* are the one wanting to succeed, those times when you are faced with the decision of watching a little more TV or going out with your friends versus finishing up some homework or studying that one concept that you know will show up on your test the next day, you will choose the latter. Recreation is certainly important to your mental health, but it must come at the right times. You must be able to focus on long-term goals when it comes down to those little decisions.

Priorities. It is a word we hear all of the time, but sometimes do not pay attention to no matter how much we think we do. But really, it all comes down to our personal priorities. Ask yourself this question: what do I want to gain through my education, and what am I willing to do to achieve it? Besides gaining knowledge to allow you to perform well in your career of choice, I'm sure you want to succeed by receiving good grades and perhaps other honors to be able to list on a résumé. However, if cheating or bribery comes to mind in order to achieve this, you've got a long way to go. On the other hand, if you truly believe you are willing to give up many things that otherwise would be important to you, then you've taken the first step into a successful and promising future. If this seems difficult for you, try to find ways to motivate yourself.

You can start your motivation process by picturing yourself five or ten years down the road. What would you really like to see yourself doing? Now picture yourself again, but this time think of what you believe you actually will be doing if you continue along your current path. Do they match? If not, try to picture the successful, improved you and make it become your future. Visualize it; hold on to it. Make it a reality. Pretend that the future you want is actually a video camera and that it really is what you will be doing.

Now that you've predicted your future, you are ready to take the steps in between now and your vision. And, of course, each step is a tiny, little, microscopic improvement. But take that little step over and over again and you'll get there. It's that simple. Make it a habit of putting your long-term goals first in your life. Then, once you have accomplished just a little bit toward your goal each day, you can feel satisfied that you are making progress.

Sure, this goal stuff is easy when you want to buy a nice car or treat yourself in some way, but it's definitely a daunting task to make school work and yucky homework a priority. Believe me. Please know that I am more against homework and school than probably anyone in the entire world. Ever since they invented the idea of wasting your precious, fun time at home with more school work, even after a long day of classes, I have been adamantly opposed to it. I've always said that I like to learn, but I just don't like school; however, I've come to realize that it's the effort that is the hard part and, really, school is set up the way it is as a result of hundreds of years of trial and error. It's probably best that way. We really do learn a whole lot because of the difficulty we have and the effort we put in. Unfortunately, that's just the way it is. So you and I must learn to live with it and make the best of it.

Through much practice and also lots of support from others, I have learned to swallow my pride and accept that school is always going to be the way it is and to do my best regardless of what I think of it. Those who know me probably would say that getting good grades is as important to me as not getting run over by a bus (which is pretty important to me, let me assure you). I eat, drink and sleep 'A's. I hate to admit that I'm probably over-motivated. The thought of not getting an 'A' makes me cringe almost as much as going to school in the first place. I'm not saying that's the frame of mind you should be in, but at least you should want to do all you can to do your best. For me, it is a wonderful reward to receive good grades after a semester of hard work, knowing that I have done my best to achieve my goals. You may very well have experienced the same thing at some point in your life. It is a great feeling to have accomplished a great task that you have set your mind to. That is my motivation. I love to succeed. I love to feel that all my time and energy was actually worthwhile. I like to look back and feel no regrets.

I've told you my motivation. This may or may not have anything to do with what motivates you to work hard. Frankly, it doesn't matter. *Find what it is that motivates you.* You know what you want. You usually know what you need to do to get it. Find those few things that make you turn off the TV in order to write that essay or to study that extra hour when necessary. It's hard. But there must be something that will remind you and motivate you to do it. It's all about getting to know yourself.

One way that you can motivate yourself is to give yourself rewards every so often. Think of leisure time, not as a top priority, but as a reward for trying hard. Start your studying *before* you entertain yourself. Once you feel that you have done enough for now, take a small break as a reward. After a little while of retreat, return to your homework. Maybe you can also enjoy a piece of candy each time you finish a math problem as a small reward for your effort. Keep going little by little. Get it done. Have some ice cream. Relax for the rest of the evening or go get some exercise or whatever it is that you like best. It will feel great! You'll be amazed at how much more enjoyable leisure time is without having the nagging feeling the whole time that you have something else you really should be doing.

Remember when your Mommy told you that you couldn't eat dessert until you finished your vegetables? The same principle applies here. Sure, dessert was the best and most enjoyable part of the meal, but it didn't give your body any long-term benefits as did the vegetables. You know how it is. It's all about discipline. Those same principles that your parents used you need to apply to yourself. It requires self-discipline to succeed and make your time and money spent on education worth it.

I would always prefer positive reinforcement to negative reinforcement when I was growing up. Though I hardly realized that I was learning discipline, I liked it when I got a special treat for doing a chore. I much preferred it to getting spanked with a wooden spoon or all of a sudden losing all of my privileges for not doing my chores. That is why you need to start to give yourself rewards early on rather than be depressed about the grade you received on your exam because you didn't study as much as you know you should have. Focus on positive reinforcement and suddenly your ugly school work will begin to be at least a little more enjoyable and you will find more success.

FRAME OF MIND

Why do you think that it would be important to have a visual picture of success? It is because the more you imagine something, the more real it becomes. If you imagine yourself as being better or smarter than you currently are, it usually becomes reality over time. It helps to build confidence, which is one of the key requirements of a great undertaking.

One of the biggest mistakes we can make concerning our education is telling ourselves that it is just not possible to achieve our goals and we are just not good enough. Believe me; I have fallen into that slump many times. But usually the mere act of allowing ourselves to think this way is the actual cause of our failure. The more we tell ourselves what we think we are, the more like that person we will become.

Believe in yourself. It's that simple. Nothing is impossible. It is very possible for a student to go from failing grades to the Honor Roll if the appropriate effort is put into it. There is nothing that can prevent that from happening more easily than having a negative attitude. Maybe some things need to be changed in order to achieve improvement. So, what are you waiting for? Make the necessary changes. That's all it takes.

It is important to realize that anything is possible. You might look at someone who seems to get an 'A' on every assignment and every test and think to yourself that you are just not capable of doing the same. Who says? Who ever told you that you weren't capable? It was probably that little negative voice inside of you that tries to tell you you're worthless. We all seem to have one. But we also have another, much more charming voice that tells us that we really are worth something and that we *can* do what we have set out to do. Unfortunately, it seems to be so much easier to pay attention to the negative voice and give up than to put in the effort to succeed.

Learn to compliment yourself. Think first about the many things you remembered when you took the test rather than the few things that you forgot. Think of your strengths before your weaknesses. Then, once you have built confidence and realize that you are capable of achieving your goals, work on your weaknesses one at a time until you have conquered them. Then is the time that you can evaluate why you forgot what you did on the test and prepare for next time so you don't make the same mistake again.

Try to remember a time in your life when you accomplished something spectacular. It may have been at a sporting event, a performance, or even something as simple as in your own home. Remember how great you felt? I'm sure you do. It was important to you; you worked hard, and you succeeded. Now, imagine a family member coming up to you, and instead of congratulating you for your success, pointing out every little thing that went wrong. Imagine that this person did not even smile or acknowledge at all how spectacular you really did, but rather scolded you because it was not perfect. What a great disappointment that would be! This is why it is so important to think positively about your successes instead of thinking only about your failures. Treat yourself the way that you would like to be treated and reward yourself for your efforts.

When thinking about our future performance, we have a strong tendency to think about past performance. If we have gotten bad grades in the past, then we think that we are going to follow that trend. Again, it is all a matter of what we believe we can do. For thousands and thousands of years, probably every human at one point had thought how great it would be to get off the ground and soar through the air. For thousands and thousands of years it seemed impossible. If Orville and Wilbur Wright had thought that since it had never been done so far that it was still impossible, they never would have attempted to fly a plane. But they believed it was possible and, sure enough, they were the first ones ever to lift off the ground in controlled flight.

If you have not performed in the past as well as you might have hoped, you need to learn to forgive yourself. After all, we all make mistakes. That was the past. You can do better. And sometimes what happened in the past was beyond our control to some degree. During my first semester in college, I was required to take English 101, which is one of my least favorite subjects. Unfortunately, I was assigned to a section where the teacher was from a distant country. Normally I wouldn't have any problem with that; however, this was quite the exception. It seemed to me that this particular teacher had begun to learn English only a month prior. Her English was terrible, and I'm sure I wasn't the only one in the class that struggled to understand a word she said. I had no idea how someone that could hardly pronounce any English in the first place was supposed to teach me better English. Nevertheless, I had no choice but to stick it out.

The first major assignment was a rhetorical analysis, which I didn't fully grasp due to my confusion in class. However, the paper was worth almost a third of my grade, so I obviously needed to at least make a worthy attempt. Considering myself a fairly good writer, I threw together an essay that I thought sounded pretty spectacular. Unfortunately, I missed the mark entirely and ended up getting a 'C' on the essay, and ultimately a 'B' in the class. Ouch. For me that was a big failure. To make a long story short, this was the only class since middle school for which I did not receive an 'A'.

But I had to learn to live with it and forgive myself. I moved on and it became a learning experience.

You're probably thinking that I could have had much worse of a failure, and that is certainly true, but to me this was a failure that I needed to overcome. Just think — that one class forever prevented me from earning a 4.0 GPA in college. There was no longer any chance; that was the hardest thing for me. I could have easily decided that since I already had one 'B', and there was no chance for a 4.0 GPA, I should no longer worry about getting 'A's. However, I did not allow myself to fall into that state of mind. There was still so much I could achieve.

Your failures may be very different, but you and I probably feel the same about them. That's what it all comes down to. We are disappointed because of our past failures. We just need to learn to overcome them and believe in ourselves. A little confidence can go a long way in helping us to achieve our long-term goals.

Another thing that is important to remember while trying to do well in school is that you need not compare yourself to others. Sometimes it does help to find out if others understand the material in order to ensure that you have a good grasp on it, but as far as performance is concerned, the only person you are competing with is yourself. Don't put yourself down because others have gotten a higher score than you. Maybe that's the only class they ever do well in. Just remember to give yourself a chance and believe in yourself, no matter what. If you perform better now than you did last time, you have succeeded.

PROCRASTINATION

This next topic is one of the deadliest killers of good grades. It seems to be a plague that lurks in every backpack, in every part of the world. It's as if it is pure human nature that given two weeks to accomplish a task, we don't get started until about 5 hours before it is due. Why is that? It's probably one of the greatest mysteries known to man.

In order to succeed, you must declare war against this deadly disease. It may not be easy, but it will be very valuable to your education. I have learned to get started on things a reasonable amount of time before they are due because I don't want to be unprepared when the deadline arrives. It is very difficult to correctly determine how much time a paper or homework assignment will take until you have started it and worked on it for awhile. It is also impossible to predict future assignments or even uncontrollable events in the near future, and if something were to come up, you would be glad that you had taken the time to do your projects early on.

Personally, I have had my share of evil teachers who

pester students by giving out the next assignment before the current one is due. Perhaps they do this in order to give us a "head start" on the next assignment in line, when in reality it just tends to add a heavier burden upon our shoulders. It seems to be a fairly common occurrence in college classes these days, so starting early may prevent you from having two unfinished assignments for any given class.

Get started. Work on all your assignments early and things will fall into place. You will discover that your burdens are not so heavy and that you really will have plenty of time to do the things that you enjoy doing. Some of my greatest memories of school were when I had gotten to an early start on my assignments and, after going at my own pace, everything was done and I had a couple of days to relax. To me, it is miraculous to feel so free, without a single burden. Of course, most of my fellow classmates viewed those last days before the due date as pure torture because all of a sudden they were faced with the reality that all of their procrastination had finally caught up with them and they would probably not get any sleep for awhile. Which would you choose?

I studied computer science in college, and in this major you can count on very large programming projects on a regular basis. As always, I would get started right away and I would find that, without all of the pressure of waiting until the last minute, they tended to get done more quickly than I might have imagined. In addition, I had time to correct mistakes if I needed to or maybe test my code a little bit more in order to make sure that everything functioned properly. In the long run, this allowed me to earn higher scores than I probably could have done otherwise. All around me, my classmates would stay up until the wee hours of the morning doing their projects the night before they were due and, predictably, later complain of fatigue and that the teacher was an idiot because they didn't get a good grade. If they had started a little earlier, I imagine they could have done better.

A few times, I even lucked out with teachers who gave extra credit for finding mistakes in their assignment write-ups. After a whole semester of starting my projects well in advance and identifying errors caused by my teachers' absent-mindedness, this added up to some pretty hefty points. It's only because I started on my projects earlier than most of my classmates that I was able to get the credit. You never can tell how much an early start will benefit you.

The stress and rush involved with last-minute effort usually tends to produce less than perfect results. Consider something as simple as a basketball game. Team A decides to come out playing their best from the start. Yeah, it's hard and it takes some endurance, but they are constantly adding points to their score. Team B, their opponent, decides that the fourth quarter is all that really matters and they'll just take their precious time for awhile. By the time the fourth quarter comes around, Team A is ahead by 30 points. Well, Team B finally comes out and puts in their effort. They realize that it's going to be an extremely difficult road to gain the victory. They are constantly fighting, doing all within their power to score. But it turns out that they are not humanly capable of performing so well in so little time. In addition, they feel so much pressure that they are unable to take good shots or even make the shots they are given. In the end, Team B loses. That is usually how it goes. A steady effort beginning early on will almost always win the prize. Decide now which team you are going to be on when it comes to your school work.

There is a phrase heard on a very regular basis on all college campuses as well as many high schools. And that phrase is "pulling an all-nighter." It is the infamous night before a major exam when all of a sudden it is crunch time. There can be no more playing around. There has been too much partying and not enough emphasis on school work. So, of course, in order to review the material one must stay up very late, if not all night, studying his or her guts out. It is hard to believe that this is such a common practice, but it's so widespread because so many people have been stung by the procrastination bug and contracted the deadly disease. But really, what does it profit to crunch all of your studying into one sleepless night? Usually your mind is not ready to handle so much information at once, especially not when it should be getting some rest instead. Experience has shown that it takes some time to actually learn and retain what you would like to memorize. So, usually the result of an all-nighter is being dead tired and getting an unsatisfactory grade. But many people continue to make it a part of their study habits and just learn to live with their mediocre performance because they really don't care too much in the first place. Are these the type of people that employers are looking for? I think not.

Another disadvantage of crunch-time studying is when you get the type of teacher that actually tests your application of concepts rather than just pure memorization. I know, it's evil, but it happens more often than you might think. These teachers know how students just look over their notes for hours at a time instead of taking time to think about the topics and actually learn them. They ask questions that you have never seen, let alone understand how they really apply. But if you have been paying attention and learning the material, you should be able to think things through and come up with a solution according to your knowledge. It's usually not that easy if your brain is tired from staying up all night, blindly reading over your notes. Again, this is another scheme that teachers have of separating the good students from the bad ones; therefore, it is important to know how to prepare so you can succeed.

It is the case that in some circumstances, things happen and there is no way around putting off some tasks given the huge load that all of your teachers have decided to pile on you all at once. No one knows better than I do the fact that every teacher feels like their class is the only one that you care about and that you would rather be doing extra loads of homework just for them because you enjoy the subject so much. The problem with this is that it doesn't mix well when every teacher is fighting for your precious time. Despite this, prioritize your tasks and get started right away on the most important ones. Learn to balance your time instead of worrying about it all later. This is one of the great skills to acquire in order to come out successful in school and in life.

GETTING TO KNOW YOURSELF

You've probably heard from hundreds of different people all kinds of tips about how to do better in school. You've probably seen people studying in many different ways, and if you've ever asked any of them why they study the way they do, they'll profess that it's the best way to remember what they're studying and that you should try it too. Maybe you've tried some of those techniques but they weren't the milk and cookies that the other students made them out to be. The point is, everyone is very different and everyone learns in a different way. It is time, if you have not done so already, to get to know yourself and how you perform best.

Studying

My wife has an interesting way of studying that, to be honest, made me think she was a little weird when I first found out. One day, when we had first started dating, we sat together in a study lounge to study for our upcoming final exams. She was studying for physiology, trying to review a whole semester's worth of bones, nerves, parts of the brain, and everything else you could possibly imagine. I quickly realized that her method of studying was extremely distracting to me. She had begun to use her hands to point out different areas on an imaginary 3D model of a human body, seemingly standing before her in the air. When possible, she would also point out various things on her own body. Not only this, but she was whispering rather loudly at the same time to help drive it home. It seemed that every time I looked down at my notes, flailing arms and hands would come into my view and I would automatically look over. Long anatomical terms that I had never heard of before began to fill my mind instead of the words I was reading in my notes. She was embarrassed when I finally asked her what in the world she was doing; she explained that it was just how she was able to memorize her notes most effectively.

From this experience, not only did I learn about my wife's interesting study habits, but I also learned a little about my own. I can't be distracted while I'm trying to study or else I won't get anything done. I have to be where it's fairly silent, away from distraction, so I can concentrate on what I'm doing. And, if I'm concentrating very hard, interruptions can blow up my temper fairly quickly. That's just the way I am. But you are probably very different. I have known people who study with loud music and the television going on at the same time and who do very well in all of their classes (though I suggest not to make this a habit). It may be that the many distractions require them to focus harder on what they're trying to remember. Who knows? I'm not an expert in that area so I can't really say; but I do know that everyone is different and it is up to each of us personally to discover how we do best and apply it to our study habits.

I have also learned through the years that I am most productive when I dedicate a good amount of time to my homework instead of completing it in short bursts and returning to it later. It seems to take me at least 15 minutes to become fully concentrated; after that time, I can roll through any task fairly easily and get a lot done in the process. If I am continuously distracted or take breaks too often, I have to waste time getting to the same level of concentration that I was at before. So, for me, it helps to make sure ahead of time that I will be able to dedicate the amount of time necessary to my studying so I can be productive. Does your mind work in the same way that mine does? Experiment! Find out what is best for you. Maybe you learn and accomplish the most when you first sit down to study. Learn to tweak your study habits in such a way that your grades can benefit in the long run.

Fatigue

I have a friend with whom I once took a linguistics class. He was in the Air Force ROTC and he usually had to get up at around 4:30 every morning to get to school before dawn in order to start his personal training and other activities. Naturally, he was very tired by the time his classes came around. I don't know how he did it, and I certainly don't condone his habits, but he would fall asleep during almost every lecture in the class we shared. I guessed that he was going to get a terrible grade and not remember anything that was mentioned by the teacher. We would study together at times to do homework or prepare for exams and, to my utter surprise, he remembered about twice as much as I did. I couldn't believe how much he could retain. I remember there were specific things that were mentioned in class during his naps that he would recall with little difficulty. I have to say, I really wish I could learn while I'm asleep. It would have made school a whole lot more fun. Unfortunately, I can't, and neither can most people.

It is a common thing to have classes fairly early in the morning and, therefore, we students have to get up earlier than we would like. For many of us, one o'clock in the afternoon is earlier than we would like. But with our busy schedules, there always seem to be times when we are a bit groggy (to put it lightly). Terribly boring teachers and movie-theater-style seats don't add to our energy levels, either. Alas, unlike my friend, most of us are not able to learn well under those conditions. We must learn to motivate ourselves and find a way to keep ourselves from slipping off into dreamland. Hopefully this doesn't involve putting a thumb-tack on our seat, but rather finding a more useful strategy to keep our minds alert and our attention level high. I have discovered through my own experience a couple of strategies that have helped me to stay awake in class.

First off, I find that taking some form of notes helps me to at least get my blood flowing a little bit. It helps me to pay attention a little more closely so I can write down important points. I have had many teachers who make it simple for us students by giving us, prior to lecture, a complete set of printed slides so we don't have to write anything down. But, more often than not, this only motivates us to shut down our brains, thinking that we already have everything that we need. I have found that even writing down some personal notes on these slides helps me to stay awake. Occasionally, I catch subtle things that are not on the provided slides, but that the teacher decides to include on a test anyway. If you think it might help you in the same way that it helps me, give it a try.

Secondly, I find that sitting a little closer to the front than usual makes me think that the teacher's looking at me and watching my every move. This is a little uncomfortable, but it's definitely not the ideal situation in which to doze off. Out of pure courtesy for your teachers, staying awake right in front them is important so as to not give the impression that they are terrible and should go jump off of a building (no matter how much you might be thinking this). Unfortunately, I've had my times when I dozed off a little and groggily opened my eyes to see my teacher staring right at me. I can say that it's not a very comfortable situation. Maybe if I had sat a little closer, I wouldn't have fallen asleep in the first place. Now, you don't have to sit in the very front row if you don't want to. When I have attempted it, I have felt so uncomfortable that I could have exploded — not to mention a little damp due to the teacher's inability to say, not spray. But as students, we have the tendency to fill up a classroom from the back row forward. Be a little daring; sit a little closer to the front than usual, and maybe it will pay off in the long run.

I only tell you my strategies to prove that I have taken the time to discover the way I am. I can still learn when I don't do these things, but making the effort to do them seems to really help me retain the things that are said in lecture. My wife likes to eat candy during lectures, where permitted, in order to stay awake. Discover the way *you* work best. It may be that sitting in the back of the classroom helps the most or just listening without taking any notes, and that's fine — as long as it truly is how you can do your *best*.

Exams

One of the most important factors in getting good grades, especially in college, is doing well on exams. This is another area of education that requires effort to get to know ourselves and how we perform best. There seems to be a frame of mind in which we all perform our best on exams.

Our bodies require a good amount of sleep and a good sleep routine. They also require energy from nutritious food, especially on the same day of an exam. We can't be too nervous or too under-confident, or else we will not be able to concentrate as well as we should. These are all definite things that *everyone* needs to do in order to perform their best. But there are some things that are different for each of us, individually, as well. One of these things is the amount of time before an exam that we begin to study. It is obviously a foolish choice to only study once, long before an exam, because by the time the exam comes around, we will probably have forgotten most things that we reviewed. It is also a foolish choice, as I have pointed out earlier, to procrastinate our studying until late the night before and compromise the amount of sleep that we receive. But each of us can find a strategy that will help us have the best frame of mind during any exam.

I have found that I usually only need to study a day or two before an exam, for a few hours. This gives me enough time to look over my notes and some parts of my textbook to help me remember what was presented in lecture. Since I have the tendency to remember a lot of what I learned in class, being someone who learns both visually and audibly, this is usually enough for me. But there have been times that I knew I needed more time studying because I had hardly understood anything in the first place. A lot of people need to study much more than this in order to retain everything. How do you need to study in order to do as well as possible on an exam? Have you discovered this yet?

It may be that you need to briefly go over your notes each day after school in order to be able to recall all of the information that you will need when you study. You may need to start studying at least a week in advance and spend several hours a day in order to do well. Or, you may be like me in that you only need a few hours of studying a day or two before an exam. The point is that you need to find a way to feel the most confident about the information on an exam without feeling overly nervous or afraid. It may take some time, but discover that balance so you can succeed. For starters, it's a good idea to begin with more studying, rather than less, as you figure out your own needs.

Many people find that if they form study groups with some of their classmates, they learn and retain the material well by actually explaining and discussing what will be on the test. This is also an excellent idea, as long as your study group is actually for studying and not just an excuse to hang out with friends; otherwise, you will more than likely find yourself wasting all of your precious study time.

You may also want to pay attention to what times and under what conditions studying is most effective for you. Do you do best when you study in the morning or in the evening? Before dinner or after dinner? Alone, or with other people? By reading, writing things out, or explaining them to someone else? When you are able to answer all of these questions, you need to apply these techniques in order to be able to perform well and be satisfied with your grade after an exam. However, when testing out different strategies to find these answers, remember that it is better to be over-prepared than under-prepared.

For many classes, teachers require students to actually memorize specific information, such as dates and names, instead of just general concepts. For exams like these, it may not be so easy to just assume that you paid attention in class and you'll do okay. Many people shudder and complain when faced with a memorization exam. But before you tell yourself that studying for these tests is extremely difficult and that you're going to have to study for weeks, let me offer some suggestions that may be useful if you find that you learn the same way that I do.

I have definitely had my share of memorization exams. The last one that I can recall was in a Roman history class. There were about 30 dates of significant battles and events in

Roman history that I needed to know for the test. I thought for a while how I could best memorize those dates without just blankly reviewing them over and over. Then I thought I'd try something new. With the dates that were listed in my notes, I began to draw directly on them. I turned, for example, a 1600 into two little soldiers with spears chasing after two others that were hiding behind shields. This signified that the date corresponded to a specific battle. I thought it seemed promising, so I went ahead and drew on the rest. Each date became a little picture relating to the event that happened during that year. As soon as I was done, I tried covering up the dates and I looked over the events one by one trying to remember the corresponding dates. To my surprise, I easily recalled every single one of them. It was great! Simply picturing the events allowed me to see the year right in front of me as if I were reading it on paper. I tried the other way around, covering up the events this time, and I remembered those as well. By doing this, I was able to transform an otherwise long and tedious evening of study into a simple, much more enjoyable time that allowed me to remember those important dates much more effectively.

Another technique that has helped me in the past was explained to me by my brother, who taught memorization techniques to high school students. It is called the "sun, shoe, tree, door, hive" method. Think of the following words: sun, shoe, tree, door, hive, sticks, heaven, gate, sign, and pen. What does this list of words remind you of? Each of these words rhymes, in order, with the numbers one through ten. When you have a memorization test that requires you to memorize a list of items or concepts in order, this method can help. What you do is associate the first item of your list with the sun. Visualize it together with the sun. If you have to remember the presidents, for example, think of George Washington tanning on the beach under the sun. Or think of anything else that comes to mind, as long as it is something you will be able to remember. Continue on down the list, associating each item with each object, in order. You'll find that if you're a visual learner at all, like I am, you will be able to easily recall your list of items, in order, by simply counting. And remember, the more wacky and crazy the visual image, the easier it will be to recall.

My wife has her own method that she uses to memorize items in order. It involves making a sentence in which each word in the sentence begins with the same letter as the item to memorize (similar to the obsolete sentence, due to Pluto's declassification as a planet, "My Very Educated Mother Just Served Us Nine Pizzas" for memorizing the planets). This is an excellent idea if you learn well using words. Or if you're poetically inclined, you could also make a rhyme, chant, or song out of what you are memorizing. My wife still remembers the quadratic formula perfectly because she memorized it to the tune of *Frère Jacques*.

Whatever your strengths are, however you learn best, find a way to apply it to your memorization. Creativity is the key. The more creative your studying becomes, the easier it will be to memorize what will be on your exam. Experiment with different methods and fine tune your own personality and strengths in order to use them to your advantage. As soon as you get to know yourself and your own strengths, you will find greater success in your classes.

Don't compromise your grades because you're lazy or unwilling to put in the effort to discover your own good study habits. Some people learn best visually; some people audibly; others by the sense of touch. Find out which of these types of people you are and adjust your way of studying and learning in order to match your personality. Unfortunately, if you don't learn best by the typical reading and lecture style that is so characteristic of our schools, you may have to come up with other ways of driving the class material into your brain. Be creative! Creativity is the key to learning and it can go a long way in the struggle to earn good grades.

TEACHERS

We must now face the unfortunate fact that we are completely dependent upon our teachers for the grades we receive in school. Even if there are teacher assistants who grade certain homework assignments and tests, it is the teacher who has the final say. Thus, it is extremely important to learn your teachers' expectations and show them that you are working hard and trying your best to be successful in their class, whether you like them or not.

Trying your best to please an exceptionally good teacher isn't all that difficult, as it usually comes quite naturally. However, when life inevitably throws you lemons and you get stuck with that repulsive teacher that you detest with all your might, being the "teacher's pet" is about as easy as shoving a banana up your nose. There will always be those teachers that just do not click with you, whether they don't know how to teach effectively, are completely ignorant of the subject they're teaching, grade unfairly, or are downright cruel to their students. In these situations, patience is of the utmost importance. Attempting to lash back at your teacher by reciprocating unkind behavior, skipping assignments, or ditching class because you are bitter will only come back to bite *you* in the end. *Always* treat your teachers with respect and dignity, and you are much more likely to earn their favor, which translates into better grades for you.

As I mentioned previously, most teachers are under the false impression that their class is the most important thing in the lives of every one of their students. They believe that even if the class is required for graduation, you have been looking forward to it your whole life and want nothing more than to be privileged with ten hours of homework relating to their class each week. It's not their problem how much other work you have to do, so why not pile it on? But even if they are merciful, usually because of having been through the same experience and understanding what a student goes through, they still want their class to have an impact on people. Good teachers usually work extremely hard to prepare for their classes and make sure that the material they present is as relevant and useful as possible. Because of this, when teachers see students who are sincerely trying their best in their class, they are willing to have some mercy when final semester grades come around.

When I begin each semester, I feel somewhat uncomfortable by the fact that my teachers do not yet know me. For all they know, I could be the worst student in the class, and it makes no difference to them whether I pass or fail. This is why I immediately take some steps to make sure that the teacher is aware that I am trying hard and my grade in the class is important to me. As soon as they know this, I feel that they will be on my side when it comes to grading my work. After all, the fact that I am taking their class seriously helps them to feel that all their work isn't in vain, which in turn will reciprocate.

Now, helping your teachers know that you are trying hard does not mean pretending to be someone you are not or acting like you care when you really don't. In order to show your teachers that you are trying hard, you must *actually* be trying hard. As we students always say, teachers have eyes in the back of their heads. Sometimes their knowledge of our effort is paranormal. Teachers can usually distinguish between the sincere students and the ones who are only acting. If you apply all of the other steps outlined in this book, you can be confident that you are trying your best and, therefore, you should take extra steps to get more involved in your class and get on your teacher's good side.

In order for the teacher to know who you are, you must draw their attention to you in a positive way. Show that you are paying attention by making eye contact and sitting up rather than slouching down on your seat as if you're about to fall off. Take some notes occasionally to show that you feel that what the teacher is saying is important. Sitting towards the front, in addition to being a good technique to help yourself stay awake, is important in order for the teacher to actually be able to see you and see that in reality you are attentive to their lecture.

Class participation, where appropriate, is also a wonderful tool. After you have paid close attention, be sure to ask questions. This will help the teacher know that you are interested in the subject and you are trying to learn the material. Many teachers often remind us that any question is a good question, and therefore we should ask anything. However, be careful that your questions are relevant and useful to others in the class. You probably shouldn't ask in front of the class why the points on your test were added up wrong or ask the teacher to repeat the information he or she just stated because you weren't paying attention. Certainly, you shouldn't ask questions such as, "Why is your nose so enormously long and pointy?" Try to make the questions as intuitive and intelligent as possible with relation to the subject at hand.

I have known many students who have asked questions that were not useful in any way. It seems that some people just have the need to be heard and will ask whatever question comes to mind. One particular individual would always ask the teacher to repeat everything he had just finished explaining, only because he wasn't paying enough to attention grasp the concept. He quickly earned himself, appropriately, the title, "The Reiterator." This type of questioning should only be used with extreme caution. It becomes burdensome and a waste of time for both the teacher and your fellow students. If you are really having trouble learning concepts and need extra help, go see the teacher on your own time and study your textbook.

I also knew someone who would ask questions about topics that were far beyond the subject matter of the class. His questions usually had no particular relevance to the basics that were being taught, but were probably for the purpose of showing off how much he already knew. Much of the time, the teachers could not adequately answer his questions, which, I am sure, added to his enormous ego. Try to limit your questions to things that have been mentioned in class or that you feel will help yourself and others to understand the important concepts. The point is not to make the teacher feel stupid because he or she can't answer questions, but rather to clarify and support the ideas on which the teacher is focusing.

It is also a good idea to add your own opinions and insights at appropriate times during lectures. If you notice something new or have a comment that will help everyone understand, don't be afraid to raise your hand and share this information. The teacher will see that you are thinking about what is being said. Nothing pleases a teacher more than to have inspired a student. If you make this inspiration known, your teacher will begin to think very highly of you and will know that you are putting forth your best effort.

Unfortunately, some classes are so large that this kind of participation is not possible. I had at least three college classes in which there were over five hundred students enrolled. The chance that your teacher will see you and remember you, let alone take a personal interest in your well being, is very slim. In these circumstances, the best way to let the teacher know that you are trying hard is to visit them during their office hours to ask for assistance. Usually, out of their entire class, only a small handful of students will come to their office during any particular semester. These names and faces the teacher is much more likely to remember. When visiting your teachers, make sure you have a good question in mind that you will be able to discuss. Most teachers are more than happy to spend some additional time helping a student to learn. However, if you go only for the purpose of getting to know the teacher, even if that's your real intent, it will be awkward and the teacher may not think that you are sincere. It will also fail to show the interest you have in learning and succeeding in his or her class. Make both your teacher's time and your time valuable and talk about something that will help you understand the material better.

Visiting your teachers during their scheduled office hours, or any time outside of class, is not only a good idea for large classes, but for any class. Office visits are not required by any means. The teacher will see that you are putting in extra time in your busy schedule *for their class*, which of course is a very touching experience for them. Not only can you gain an extra advantage when it comes to class material, but you can have one-on-one time to get to know the teacher a little bit better. This can come in very useful when in the future you need letters of recommendation for continuing your education or getting that job you always wanted. You never know when you will need them, and there are very few teachers, if any, that will give their word about the good working habits of a student that they don't remember or have never really been acquainted with.

Sometimes it is not possible to visit teachers in their office because of conflicting schedules or other reasons. However, most teachers usually provide alternative means of contacting them. It is usually possible for students to schedule appointments outside of office hours when necessary. Also, with the rise in importance of the Internet in current schools, most teachers provide an email address as an additional source of contact. Be sure to take advantage of these alternatives when available if you are not able to talk to your teachers otherwise.

Regular attendance and punctuality is also very important in giving the teacher a good impression of your effort. A student that is never seen in class is a student, as most teachers assume, that is not interested in his or her grade. Walking in late to every class is not a good idea either, because it is distracting and irresponsible. If there are circumstances that prevent punctuality, such has having to walk across campus between classes, talk to the teacher early on so he or she is aware of your circumstances if you arrive late occasionally. You don't want to draw any negative attention to yourself.

It is also important to go the extra mile in your assigned work. Put forth a good effort on your homework assignments. Do extra credit work when it is available. Volunteer for various activities in class and answer questions posed by the teacher. These will all be of benefit to you. It's almost as if each teacher keeps a running score of each of the positive and negative things that he or she sees you do. Try to make sure that the positive points and the effort highly outnumber the negative, and your teacher will have an overall good impression of you.

One last, but important, detail is to never cheat. We will get more into this later, but for now, remember that you want your teacher to trust you. Do not give them any reason to suspect that the paper you turned in was not your own work or that you wrote the answers to your test on the palm of your hand or the brim of your hat. Trust is one of the most important things that you should try to gain when getting to know your teachers. Once you have it, do not violate that trust or it will be very difficult to earn it again.

One of the main benefits of getting to know your teachers is when you have ended up with a borderline grade after a semester of hard work. This is when it really comes down to the teacher's judgment what grade you deserve. This is the culmination of the whole semester and what the teacher remembers of you and your "score" that has been added up in his or her mind. Were you always working hard and participating in class, or did you constantly show up late or not at all and put in mediocre effort? No matter how objective your teacher's grading system might seem, most teachers are willing to either raise or lower your grade depending on their opinion of you and your study habits.

Even your toughest teachers will occasionally show some mercy when it comes to your grade. In one of the hardest classes I have ever taken, I ended up with what officially was 88% for the semester. This percentage was clearly out of range of being rounded up to an 'A'. But, using the scores I had received and following the grading policies, the grade I added up for myself was over 90%. I obviously was concerned about this and wanted to bring it up to my teacher. Unfortunately, he was one of the least personable people I had ever met. He had never once greeted anyone in class, smiled, or made anything interesting. He simply stood, solid as a tree and poker-faced, at the front of the classroom until the class officially began, at which point he immediately dove into the lecture material.

I had been to class every day, though, and had made an effort to participate during the few opportunities afforded to me. I had also been to his office on one occasion to inquire about a missed test question that I thought I had answered correctly. In that class, each homework assignment had an extra credit question that was ridiculously difficult. Even so, I attempted every one and usually earned some points for my effort.

One day, I communicated my concern by email and he immediately responded. His explanation of why my grade calculation came out differently than I expected was that the extra credit did not actually count for anything, except on extreme borderline grades that were within half of a percentage point. We proceeded to "converse" by email over the next few minutes, during which time I explained that I was not aware of this and that I had done my best in the class. He again looked over my grade and told me, "Okay, you've done all the extra credit, which wasn't required, and it looks like you've worked hard. I'll give you an 'A'." What an ecstatic moment for me! Something I had done to show him that I was trying hard all semester obviously paid off.

Learn to use your teachers and their power to determine grades to your advantage. It will certainly be of benefit to you. If they see that you are giving your all and, of course, they know your name so they can apply your efforts to your grade, you are much more likely to succeed in these situations. Make it a habit of doing this, no matter how inconvenient it may be or how much you truthfully dislike your teacher.

TRACKING YOUR GRADE

Relating the experience with my less-than-personable teacher brings me to another important point I would like to make: you can't always trust your teacher to keep track of your grades perfectly. You need to take part in calculating your grades as well. Teachers are usually willing to provide a list of all the scores you have earned during a particular semester, to which you can compare those that are written on assignments and exams. If nothing else, they should be able to provide you with a current percentage grade that you can use in comparison with your own calculation. But all too often students just look at their calculated grade, accept it, and never take the time to verify that it's correct.

It's easy to think that teachers are in perfect control of your grades. In reality, teachers often have hundreds of students to keep track of and, even though they try to enter scores correctly, they sometimes come up short. If I were entering my own grade into a grading program or spreadsheet, I would probably check the data about three times, type it carefully, erase it if it didn't *feel* right, rewrite it, and proceed to verify in order to be fully sure that it was entered correctly. Teachers aren't necessarily this careful.

Make it a habit of comparing your official grade to that which you expect to be earning. I can't count the number of times that there have been incorrect entries in my teachers' records. Sometimes these errors have had a big impact on my overall scores. Nobody is perfect, and when entering grades late at night or while there are distractions, it is certainly not impossible for your teachers to enter your grades incorrectly. If these errors are never spotted, you may unknowingly receive an unfair final grade.

If you do find discrepancies, don't be afraid to *politely* approach your teacher about them. If there are any errors, your teacher will usually be happy to correct them. If not, doing so gave you a chance to come in contact with your teacher and he or she will now know that you are concerned with success and that you are serious about the grade you receive. It is a win-win situation.

To illustrate the fact that teachers make mistakes with their grading, I once had a Spanish grammar class in which I performed exceptionally well. Having lived in Puerto Rico for two years and studied intense grammar, I pulled off the entire semester without losing a point on anything. I received 100% on every homework assignment, paper, and test. It was a hole in one. Never had any class gone so extremely smoothly. I even earned every possible extra credit point, which was many. But when the end of the semester came along, the teacher reported that I had about 98% instead of the overly perfect score that I had expected. I could not understand why it was so much lower than it should have been. It would have been ridiculous to contest my grade in this case, since the discrepancy made absolutely no difference on my transcript, but obviously a few important scores were omitted. If I had instead earned 89%, imagine how much those two percentage points would have been worth! This is why it is important to keep track of your grade and defend it when necessary.

I also can't stress enough the importance of reviewing your exams and homework assignments, after they are graded, in order to determine why you received the scores that you did. First of all, it is just good practice because you will be able to learn from your mistakes. The things that you miss on an exam will stick out in your mind like a crocodile among a flock of baby chicks. If you never find out what you did wrong, you will never be able to correct it for future exams. Secondly, I have lost count of how many times my assignments and tests were graded incorrectly. This is usually because the teachers' assistants do a lot of the grading, they are hardly ever in class, and usually only qualify to be assistants because they took the class at one point and earned a reasonable grade. But that certainly doesn't mean that they know everything. They usually grade your work by comparing it to the teachers' answers, but they may not necessarily understand other ways that problems can be solved correctly.

One particular example was of extreme importance for my grade. It was a fairly difficult 400-level college course dealing with computer networking. The first test turned out to be unexpectedly math-oriented and proved very difficult for almost everyone in the class. I was shocked to see my grade, 31 out of 50. My score on an associated homework assignment, which was returned to me at the same time, was horrific as well. I could have just lived with it and moved on, even though it was worth a large portion of my grade, but I decided to take a closer look at it later that day to see what had gone wrong. It was a good thing I did. On most of the problems that I had missed, there was a particular conversion for which I had used an exact value in order to be as accurate as possible. However, it turned out that my teacher had used a mere estimation to do his calculations. I took my test to him during office hours that week and talked to him about it. Of course, since he wasn't really involved in grading the exams, he had to look it over for himself to determine how I had approached each problem. It turned out that he agreed that it was graded wrong and I earned back 26% on my test! My score went from a low D to a high B just because I had talked to him and made a claim about my work and why I felt it was correct. He also significantly raised my homework score due to the same grading error. In light of that experience, I definitely condone the practice of verifying the grades that you receive.

I recommend talking to your teacher whenever you feel that something was graded incorrectly. It is your right as a student to make sure that your grade is fair. Even if the things you contest were actually graded correctly, the fact that you can defend your answers will sometimes earn you partial credit and provide some help for your overall grade.

If it is the case that you don't know why a problem was incorrect and you can't figure it out yourself, go to your teacher anyway or at least talk to a fellow student and see if it can be explained to you. It will help you learn and will allow you to correct your mistakes in the future. After all, problems that are commonly missed on midterms and homework assignments are usually very likely to appear on final exams. You will be glad that you took the time to keep track of your grades.

COMPLETENESS

When I mention completeness, I mean to say that it is necessary to fulfill all obligations in each class. By obligations I mean attendance, class participation, and assignments. These are important factors in the amount that you will learn in a class and, therefore, they are also important in your performance on exams. Additionally, they are often a direct portion of your grade. That is why you need to know how your grade will be calculated and what will be weighted the most heavily in order to build up your grade in those areas. However, not only the most heavily weighted portions of your final grades are important for each class, but also the tiny grades that you may feel don't make much of a difference.

Attendance

In my high school, those who had perfect attendance had the chance to be rewarded fairly heavily. At the end of every quarter, all those students who had had perfect attendance for that quarter were entered into a drawing to win prizes such as used cars or jewelry. Since I was driving the most atrocious, broken down, worn-out vehicle many people had ever seen, attending classes as much as possible seemed to be worth the effort. I had perfect attendance throughout high school. Unfortunately, despite all of the chances I had, I never won anything. I felt quite cheated that I was never able to be rewarded for my effort. But, looking on the bright side, I feel that going to class all the time helped me to stay caught up with important material and follow along more easily. I have learned throughout the years that even though there is a textbook or printed notes that one can refer to for any particular class, what the teacher says in class is usually what will be emphasized on exams. It is important to be present so as to not miss out on subtle comments that will help you know what will be expected of you.

To be completely honest, I probably would have had perfect attendance even if there were no prizes for doing so. In fact, I had almost perfect attendance in middle school just because I wanted to. But it is important to note the purpose of my motivation. I did not go to class all the time to be a freak or a teacher's pet or even because I liked school (which is the excuse of many perfect-attendance students, but obviously not mine). My main motivation was actually based on my hatred of unnecessary homework and time spent on school related material outside of school. I have always hated homework with a passion, and by going to class all the time, I didn't have to make up any material or assignments. It probably takes the average student twice as long to catch up on material manually than if he or she had attended class in the first place. And, if not caught up by the next lecture, it may put him or her behind even more because of not being able to understand the additional material. And this all goes without mentioning the fact that assignments and tests will have to be made up where necessary. All in all, it is a big time-saver to just go to class when you are supposed to.

The prevention of extra effort may motivate you as it motivates me. I always try to find ways that I will personally benefit from doing something. Most importantly, good attendance will benefit your grade because you will be caught up on the material and ready to learn more by building on what you currently know. If you have gone to class but still didn't quite understand what was taught, be sure to go over your notes or your textbook if necessary. Do what you need to before each class to feel that your understanding level is where it should be.

Aside from the indirect benefits of attending class, I have encountered countless teachers who use attendance as some percentage of the final grade in order to reward those who come to class. This is a simple, yet important way to add some points to your score. Don't take these points lightly; they could make all the difference in your grade if it ends up on one of those infamous borderlines.

Class Participation

I have mentioned participation in class as a good way for the teacher to know that you are putting forth an effort to learn. But again I mention it in order to cover the possibility of a participation grade. The highest weight I have seen is 20%; with stakes this high it is very important to participate as much as is necessary. Make sure you know what the teacher expects of you for participation. A few weeks into a semester it is good practice to ask your teacher if he or she feels that you are participating enough in class. This is usually a good indication of what you will need to do the rest of the semester in order to secure full participation credit.

For many people, the participation grade is very difficult. In any given class, there are usually only a handful of people who regularly participate. This may be due to the fear of saying the wrong thing or because of pure timidity. Nearly everyone has fear of speaking in public to some extent and will have to put forth an effort to participate. If you are the type of person who has a serious problem with any kind of class participation due to an excessive amount of shyness, it may be worth letting the teacher know ahead of time. Many times, teachers are willing to provide an alternative means of securing participation points. In the class that I had where participation was 20% of the final grade, the teacher created online forums where students could go to discuss material. By posting three messages per week, the teacher awarded the full points as if these things were discussed in class.

Group participation is also a must. Teachers usually keep an eye on students when they are working as a group. In fact, it is one of the few times that a teacher has a chance to take their focus away from what they are going to say next and, instead, simply observe what is going on in the classroom. If you are taking part, consider yourself the recipient of some simple, yet valuable points.

Assignments

Assignments are usually the most heavily weighted portion of your grade. This is done in part as an act of kindness because I don't know too many people who would like their grades to be based solely on a couple of tests throughout a semester. Assignments pad your grade very nicely, even if they are worth only a few points. Again, I have pointed out earlier that doing all of your assignments is an indication to your teacher that you are trying your best and also a good way to keep yourself caught up in class. But, again, I must mention that they bear a direct influence on your grade as well.

It is human nature to be lazy sometimes and think, "I probably don't need to do this assignment; after all, it's only worth a few points and I want to do something else tonight." But many times your grade comes down to those few missed points that you didn't think were necessary. As soon as you begin to rationalize that you'll be able to get along just fine without those points, it will become more of a habit later on. Always consider the worst-case scenario; imagine yourself at the end of the semester, lacking only a few points to get the grade that you wanted all along. At that point, do you think your attitude will be different towards that skipped assignment? Do the assignment now in order to prevent that from happening at all.

Some teachers allow one or two homework grades to be dropped at the end of the semester. If this is the case, do not skip assignments early on. Complete every one the best that you can so that the lowest grade can be dropped. It may be the case that the assignment at hand seems like it will be the hardest and you skip it, only to discover that worse ones lie ahead. You'll be in the very best shape, and have the most peace of mind, if you do your best on every one. Decide at the end of the semester, when you can see the whole picture, where to use your "free passes."

In some classes, assignments are so valuable to the final grade that there is no way you would dare to not complete an assignment. At those times, it is very important to try your best. Read each question carefully and make sure you understand it well before continuing. A misunderstanding, though it may be a common one, will not earn you points. If you do not have any clue as to how to approach a homework problem and you have taken the necessary steps such as asking your teacher or TA for assistance, do not just leave the problem blank. There is no better way to guarantee zero points for such a problem. Most teachers award partial credit for effort, even though a problem is incomplete or not fully correct. At least write down what you know to be true. I usually go to the next step and try to manipulate what I know into some kind of answer as if I know what I'm doing. I'm wrong more often than not in those cases, but half credit on a problem is much better than zero credit.

Some assignments are very important to our grade even if we don't quite realize it. I once had a class where the assignments were only worth five points each. I didn't take them quite as seriously as I could have. The main problem was that the teacher never announced when we had assignments or when they were due. We always had to take a look at our syllabus in order to know. Sometimes I completely forgot to read my syllabus, and I would get to class and see everyone turning in their completed assignments. So in the five minutes before class started, I frantically completed my homework and turned it in. Since it was a class of five-hundred students, the teacher could hardly have cared if homework was done at the last minute. However, I am very glad that I turned in the homework instead of just blowing it off because, as it turned out, those five points that each assignment was worth were actually heavily weighted. I had no idea that it was counted as such an important part of my grade. It just goes to show that no matter how insignificant your homework may seem, you might find that it is much more important than you think.

CLASSMATES

One thing I wish I would have done more throughout my school career is get to know my fellow classmates. Typically, I would go to class and hardly talk to anyone, anxiously awaiting the chance to dart out quickly when class time finally ended. I was always more comfortable having fun with friends than being stuck in a boring classroom full of strangers. However, I realize now that most of my classes would have been much more enjoyable had I taken the time to make friends with those around me. Not only that, but it would have given me more opportunities to study and discuss class material with fellow classmates.

It is much easier for me to participate in class when I am surrounded by familiar people. If I have friends to talk to, it makes me feel much more like I am a part of the class and much of the awkwardness of making comments or asking questions is relieved. Also, if I have missed a brief comment from the teacher, I can turn to my neighbor to copy notes or to ask a quick question instead of having to disrupt the teacher and the rest of the class because of my attention lapse.

There have been many times when I have felt that studying in a group setting would have helped me prepare much more effectively for a test, but I did not know anyone in my class well enough to organize a study group. It would have been nice to always have that backup. As I have mentioned earlier, study groups are extremely effective for some people; explaining and discussing is one way that people can learn and retain information fairly quickly. If you have gotten to know your classmates ahead of time, study groups can be more easily formed.

It is also a good idea to collect contact information, such as an email address, from several of your classmates at the beginning of a term. When you are not able to attend class or you need help with certain concepts, you can contact them and ask what you have missed, borrow their notes, or simply just ask them to explain what they know about a topic. This is not something you could request from a complete stranger half-way through the semester.

During the first few days of classes is when you need to break out of your comfort zone to introduce yourself to your neighbors. Most people won't think you are strange for wanting to get to know them; instead, they may have thought about introducing themselves to you but didn't have the courage to do so. If you miss the opportunity to get to know some of your classmates during the first week of a semester, it will be much more difficult and awkward later on, after you have all seen each other during every class but haven't yet taken the time to communicate.

If you are lucky enough to have good friends who have registered for the same classes, this prevents the awkwardness of not knowing anyone in your class at the beginning of the semester. However, it can either help or hurt your grade in the long run. When students sit next to their long-time friends, there is much more of a tendency to spend class time talking about significant others or whatever other topic is on their minds rather than paying attention to the lecture. If you feel that you won't be able to get anything done around one of your friends, it is probably not a good idea to plan your schedules together in the first place. In order to use class time effectively, it is very important that you know when to talk and when to pay attention. If you use your class time wisely, then having a good friend by your side can be very beneficial, as you will be able to discuss important points or study together before an exam. If nothing else, it will help relieve some of the stress of being a full-time student.

Finally, some teachers often enjoy providing projects that are to be completed in a small group or partner setting. Sometimes you get to choose your group and sometimes you do not. One of the most difficult situations in group settings is when one or more of the group members does not put forth any effort to participate or complete his or her part. This has happened to me far too many times. I have the tendency to take the lead of the group if no one else immediately steps in, and I usually end up having to do most of the work because some of the members fail to do all that is expected of them. This can be very frustrating. When you have group projects and you feel that one or more of the group members is not participating, it is very important that you let your teacher know. If you are trying hard to get good grades and someone in your group couldn't care less about their own grade, the last thing that you should want to happen is to let their negativity and laziness pull down your own grade. If you have told the teacher with enough anticipation, arrangements can usually be made to benefit you.

ORGANIZATION

It seems like everyone has a different way of organizing their stuff. What one person thinks is an organized desk may appear to others as a mess of papers and books. But the purpose of organization is so we can find what we need when we need it. If we can't, then we have not properly organized our belongings.

If you are the type of student who regularly forgets about homework assignments and tests or who on repeated occasions has been unable to find homework when it was due, it is time to consider a better method of organization. Open up your backpack or whatever it is that you use to carry your books and supplies. Is there a space designated for papers from each class, be it a folder, binder, accordion file, etc.? Can you distinguish between papers from this week and papers from several months ago? Are there fuzzy creatures living in the unknown depths within?

It is important that every item have its designated place. There must be a place for both notes and handouts for each class. These could be in the same area or in different areas, depending on how you are most comfortable. In my backpack, I tend to keep a three-ring binder with tabbed dividers where my notes for each class are kept. I can add more sheets of paper as necessary, since some classes require many more notes than others. I also utilize a separate zippered division of my backpack to hold several two-pocketed folders, which is where I store handouts and homework pertaining to each class. They are all different colors, and at the beginning of each semester I decide which color corresponds to which class and I remember it throughout the semester. For me, this is the easiest way to organize my things (that, and the fact that the three-ring binder was a gift and I thought I might as well use it). Another option is to have a spiral notebook for each class, possibly with slots on each cover where you can store your handouts. Whatever you choose, make sure that it will provide a way for you to remember where your important items are for each class and give you easy access to those items.

Even beyond the physical folders and binders, I have additional ways of keeping my papers organized in my mind. Typically, I use the left side of my folders for papers that are older, such as tests and homework assignments that have been returned or handouts that are no longer applicable to the current focus of a class. On the right side, I keep up-to-date and relevant items such as current handouts and completed homework assignments that I am yet to turn in. I also try to keep my papers somewhat in a new-to-old order as much as possible. I find this method very useful because I can open up a folder and easily find what I need without having to search through an entire stack of papers. Try to pay attention to details such as these when you organize. You may want to utilize my strategies or you can be creative and come up with your own, if you have not already done so. If your papers are organized well, you are less likely to forget about homework, etc., because you will know where relevant information is kept.

Another organization issue that is worth mentioning is that of remembering important events. We students are often bombarded with test dates and due dates from all directions. It is very important, as far as our grades are concerned, to be able to remember these dates. I am typically able to remember dates easily because when an important date is mentioned, it is immediately shoved into my "stress-out-because-I-don't-want-that-day-to-arrive" area of my brain. Once it reaches that point, it is almost impossible to forget. But if you don't have a crazy, wacky mind like I do, then you may need to write some things down in a more permanent medium.

There are several different options for organizing your upcoming events. Those living in the high-tech world may want to purchase an electronic organizer, be it a PDA, cell phone, or even just computer software in order to maintain a calendar and to-do list. Whatever the device, it can most likely be configured to provide sounds and pop-up alerts as reminders that will drive everyone else crazy. If your brain isn't a computer, it may be more helpful for you to get a daily planner in which you can write things down when necessary. Or, if you think it is sufficient, simply write down important dates and other information on a piece of paper or note card that you can refer to often. The main requirement is that you have a central area that you can refer to when you need to know what is coming up. This is a necessary improvement to writing down dates in all sorts of places that you will have to search through later.

Now is the time to get organized. Give these strategies a try if you haven't incorporated them already and see if your grades don't begin to improve. It certainly can't hurt your grades; at the least, it will provide you with valuable skills that will be much more useful to you later on in life.

WRITING SKILLS

It's tough to estimate exactly, but school is composed of a handful of different areas from which we are judged. If I had to give an average estimate, this would be the breakdown of the different areas of schoolwork: 5% luck, 10% oral, 20% intelligence and ability, 25% effort, and **50% writing**. Yes, that's right, 50% writing; at the very least. Just think about it for a minute…homework is almost always written, so are tests, essays, research papers, etc. Even oral presentations in class usually involve some sort of paper that must be distributed to the teacher and your classmates. Proper spelling, grammar, and clarity are important in all courses, not just English class.

In my opinion, 99% of writing for school purposes is completely boring, usually because of the nature of the subject on which the writing is based. It's just one of those things that you have to suck up and do just because you have to. But if you hate written assignments as much as I do (and hopefully you don't), please do not let this negatively impact how well you write. It makes up such a huge portion of your grade that you just cannot afford anything less than your best effort.

Paying attention to detail can go a long way for your grade. When you write a paper, do you ever read it once you're through? This is one of the best habits you can have when it comes to your writing skills. No matter how good of a writer you think you are, you will be amazed at the amount of changes that need to be made after your first pass of revision. I have always considered myself to be a fairly competent writer (though you may be thinking otherwise). I have always been a phenomenal speller and practically a grammatical genius, for the sake of exaggeration. But I have found in my many years of schooling that the extra fifteen minutes required to look over my paper once more has really been a benefit to my grade.

Another suggestion: use your computer's spelling and grammar check! Not only that, use your own spelling and grammar check, A.K.A. your brain, since the computer isn't always right. Spelling and grammar errors stand out to teachers like snow in the desert. Think of all the papers they have to read every time an assignment is due; in addition, they have usually been doing this same job for a very long time. To put it in street slang, they know what's up. If you have cleaned up your spelling and grammar mistakes the best that you can, your teacher can focus more on the good grade that he or she is planning to give you. The less the strain of trying to make sense of what you wrote, the less red marks there are on your paper, the better the teacher's impression of your effort, and the better your grade. That is the golden equation.

Don't always trust suggestions made by peers when they review your work. Don't get me wrong, peer reviews can work wonders and are a great tool when necessary. But usually they are required and the other students are graded based on the fact that edits are physically written on the paper. I'm sure you understand the feeling of caring more about your own grade than others' grades. Perhaps you've had times in your life, like me, where you made a suggestion on someone else's paper that really wasn't all that important, but you wrote it anyway in hopes of impressing the teacher with your editing skills. Read the suggestions that other people make, and by all means correct those areas that are clearly mistakes, but when you incorporate others' suggestions into your work, make sure it is your work; in other words, ensure that each edit fits the context, meaning, and flow of your writing the way you intended it. Otherwise it may end up being detrimental to your overall composition and your grade.

Finally, be absolutely sure that you know what you are supposed to write about. Remember my rhetorical analysis in English 101? I sure do. That one paper killed my perfect GPA, for life. But in hindsight, I realize that I did poorly because I did not fully understand what it was that I was writing about. Writing a paper that's off topic is like taking penicillin in order to relieve a headache: it just won't work, no matter how powerful it may be. Nothing is more harmful to your grade on a writing assignment, essay question on an exam, etc., than to entirely miss the point. Take some extra time to think ahead and focus on your topic before you waste your efforts on nonsense.

INTEGRITY

Don't cheat! You may think that it's a wonderful way to get past a class easily and without consequence. But you may someday realize that the seemingly unimportant subject in which you cheated is the very thread by which your employment hangs. You will surely regret it in the future. Please, don't do it, don't consider it, and don't support it, whether or not you think your teacher will catch you or even care. What if your dentist or surgeon had cheated on his or her tests or papers in school? Would you continue to be their patient?

Don't plagiarize! Yes, writing is important, but you must develop your writing skills on your own. I know of people who were expelled from college in their last semester for plagiarism. All of their time, money, and dreams of graduation were wasted because of one paper for which they decided to "borrow" someone else's words without attributing the proper credit.

Even if you can get away with cheating or plagiarism,

you will regret it in the future. Were you aware of the fact that college degrees can be revoked? It's true; you may be able to cheat your way through medical school and your dissertation, for example. But if and when it is determined that you cheated, your license and degree can be revoked, jeopardizing your employment and the respect of your colleagues.

If the thought of the distant future isn't enough to make you more honest, then think of the present. Though you may feel that you're immune to getting caught, the chance that you will is an awfully hot fire to play with. Aside from getting a low or no score for the assignment or exam, you risk being expelled from school, especially if you're in college. This is certainly a possible consequence, as I have observed.

Basically, avoid cheating like it is a deadly plague…one that can kill your grade and your future.

CONCLUSION

I have now spilled my guts. All of my secrets are now exposed; consider yourself lucky. I have shared a lifetime of experience in one compact, easy to read guide so you don't have to walk in the dark. I just hope that my advice will help you in some way to unleash the remarkable student that's longing to escape. A lot of my advice will require some significant effort to incorporate into your study habits, but the effort is necessary if your goals are to be attained.

In summary, I would like to review with you the smart way to earn better grades in school:

- Motivate yourself
- Visualize success
- Don't procrastinate
- Get to know yourself and what study habits help you learn the most effectively
- Know your teachers and find ways to let them know that you are working hard
- Monitor your grade throughout each semester

- Fulfill all your obligations for each class
- Interact positively with your classmates
- Keep yourself well organized
- Focus on writing skills
- Do not cheat or plagiarize

Now, after all is said and done, I must wish you good luck. I truly hope that you will begin to see a significant improvement in your grades in the near future because of your efforts to incorporate better learning strategies. You have come far enough in your pursuit of success to purchase and read this book; do not let it end here. Put these tips into good practice and you will be well on your way to a path of great success; not only in school, but in your lifelong pursuits as well.

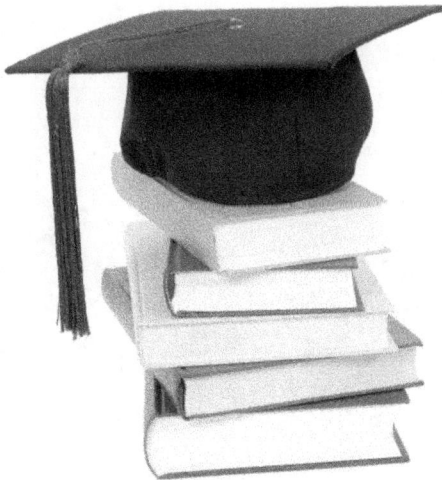

About the Author

Chris James was born and raised in Prescott, Arizona. He graduated from Prescott High School with honors and a 4.0+ GPA. He continued his education by attending The University of Arizona, where he completed his bachelor's degree in Computer Science with a minor in Spanish, achieving a 4.0 major and minor GPA and a *summa cum laude* honor designation in December, 2005. He was also selected as the Outstanding Senior for the UA Department of Computer Science and nominated as the Outstanding Senior for the UA College of Science. Other accomplishments include the Boy Scouts of America Eagle Scout award and 2-year full-time missionary for The Church of Jesus Christ of Latter-day Saints. He is currently living with his wife, Melanie, in Tucson, Arizona and is excelling as a Software Engineer for a major defense contractor.

www.ingramcontent.com/pod-product-compliance
Lightning Source LLC
Chambersburg PA
CBHW021217020426
42331CB00003B/351